Victorian Découpage

TEDDY BEARS

CAXTON EDITIONS

This edition first published in the United Kingdom in 2001 by
Caxton Editions
20 Bloomsbury Street
London WC1B 3JH
a member of the Caxton Publishing Group

Designed and Produced for Caxton Editions by
Open Door Limited
Rutland, UK

Découpeur and professional advisor: Sue Growcott, Chez Soi Ltd, Stamford
Illustrator: Andrew Shepherd, Art Angle
Teddy Bear Photography: Michael Pearson
Product Photography: Chris Allen, Forum Advertising

Colour separation: GA Graphics Stamford

Title: Victorian Découpage, TEDDY BEARS
ISBN: 1-86019-965-8

Acknowledgments:
All the Teddy Bears featured in this publication were reproduced by the kind permission of
Sue Pearson, Antique Dolls and Teddy Bears
13½ Prince Albert Street, Brighton BN1 1HE, East Sussex
Website www.sue-pearson.co.uk

Contents

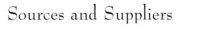

The Classic Bear ◇════════════

Wherever I am, there's always Pooh,
There's always Pooh and Me.
Whatever I do, he wants to do,
'Where are you going to-day?' says Pooh:
'Well, that's very odd 'cos I was too.
Let's go together,' says Pooh, says he.
'Let's go together,' says Pooh.

A. A. Milne

A. A. Milne's 'Us Two', from his classic poetry collection Now We Are Six effortlessly describes the closeness between a young child and his teddy bear. Milne knew all about bears. Winnie the Pooh, his most famous creation – a lovable, roly-poly sort of a bear, a bit battered about the ears, worn in places by much loving, a friend who was always there – was based on the bear that belonged to his son 'Christopher Robin'.

During the 1920s London was taken by storm by an American Black Bear called Winnie that had newly arrived from the United States and had taken up residence in London Zoo. Milne and his son visited the bear on several occasions, along with thousands of others, and in December 1925 he introduced the world to his very own Winnie-the-Pooh. He would become the most famous and loved bear in literature.

Pooh may have been 'a bear with little brain', but his appeal was universal. He was part of an increasing family, which was spreading across all the continents of the world into the homes of rich and poor, adults and children. And while Germany and the United States argued over paternity of the prodigious child, the teddy bear kept gaining in popularity.

If you go down to the woods today be sure of
a big surprise,
If you go down to the woods today you'd
better go in disguise,
For every bear that ever there was,
Will gather there for certain because,
Today's the day the teddy bears have their
picnic.

So wrote the English lyricist Jimmy Kennedy. Teddies had taken over the world. Nowhere was safe!

According to popular legend, Theodore Roosevelt, the 26th president of the United States, was the man who gave rise to the teddy bear. But while Roosevelt may have ignited the spark of the idea – following a hunting incident with a bear in 1902 – he was by no means fond of the subsequent cuddly toy. In fact it was said he actively disliked the furry creatures. However, it was the Roosevelt story that provided the inspiration for Brooklyn entrepreneur Morris Michtom to make a stuffed bear with movable arms and legs. At roughly the same time, in Germany, a small family firm of toy makers hit upon the same idea. The Steiff Company's bear

was, at first, slow to capture the public imagination, but by 1910 sales had rocketed and a US market secured.

Many of the earliest teddies to enter the British market were Steiff bears. But UK manufacturers were soon to follow suit. The fashion caught hold on both sides of the Atlantic and by the First World War teddies were appearing in books and on postcards and Christmas cards. They were popular scraps too.

Some of the most charming postcards of this period were designed by Mabel Lucie Attwell, whose endearing chubby-faced children were inevitably accompanied by plump little bears. Donald McGill, the saucy seaside postcard artist, also had a penchant for the bear.

Bears were not just pictured as the child's best friend though. They could be seen playing golf, ice-skating, sailing toy boats and sipping tea. They also turned into policemen, airplane pilots, and concert pianists.

The love affair with the teddy bear has continued. Winnie-the-Pooh was joined in 1956 by a somewhat bedraggled character in a shabby duffel coat who had come all the way from darkest Peru. His name was Paddington and today his story is a children's best-seller.

Another best-seller is Rupert Bear, who first appeared as a cartoon-strip in the British national newspaper the Daily Express in 1920. Still popular today, he now has his own fan club, the Rupert League, with members around the world.

Introduction

Derived from the French word découper, which means 'to cut out', découpage is the art of decorating with cut out shapes, patterns and pictures. The cut-outs are glued to a suitable surface and subsequently varnished many times. With careful work and a little patience the cuttings and surface unite to create a new and convincing object.

Be it homespun or exquisite, necessity or sheer indulgence, découpage is engaging, addictive even. Of necessity its practitioners become collectors and hoarders. One dare not throw anything away. A print which appears dull and uninteresting in isolation may be just what is needed to offset another which is lively and bold. The success of a project depends as much on how the images are combined and set out as it does on the dexterity of the cutting and quality of the finishing.

Découpage can be delicate and painstaking or it can be simple and direct. It might be just something to fill a wet afternoon or a grand statement of taste and style. Whatever form a project takes, your creation will be unique. Given the same source material no two people will produce the same object. Découpage recycles and reinvigorates mass-produced images to produce one-offs.

Like so much else, the roots of découpage are to be found in the East. Paper making originated in China 2,000 years ago and from that followed paper cutting. When the East India Company opened trade routes to the East, European eyes could scarcely believe the beauty of Oriental lacquerwork.

Demand for this wonderful coloured and highly finished furniture led artists and artisans all over Europe to experiment with

their own styles and techniques throughout the nineteenth century.

There was money to be made. Not a trick was missed. So it was that in the hothouse workshops and arteliers of Venice, Paris and later London, that a new decorative art form was born.

Frustrated by the cost and time involved in working with paint and gold leaf, master painters engaged apprentices to colour, cut and manipulate their original engravings and etchings. Early in his career the Rococo artist François Boucher worked as an engraver for Watteau, who in turn had studied in Venice.

Gradually the new art slipped away from the masters. By the time of Louis XVI lesser artists such as Pillement had carved out a very successful niche. Chinoiserie was much in vogue with the ladies of the French court. Hour upon hour was spent perfecting scissor-work. Throughout the eighteenth century découpage flourished all over Europe and all the while, as printed material became cheaper to produce more and more people were able to try their hand.

It is no surprise that the Victorians fell so much in love with this art. The Industrial Revolution forged a new world of mass-production. What the old masters had come to dismiss as arte povera (poor man's art) could now in a sense fulfil its destiny. Newspapers and magazines brought about an explosion of printed material. Images were more widely available than ever before.

Découpage was the perfect Victorian pastime. It brought together many character-istics of the age – the mania for collecting, a certain sense of thriftiness and an overarching sentimentality which saturated the public imagination.

Queen Victoria herself kept a scrapbook as did many millions of her subjects. All across the Empire, ladies eagerly gathered the popular images of the day – hearts and flowers, birds, angels, children and cats.

This book introduces the novice to the Victorian art of découpage. Each book in the Victorian Découpage series spotlights a subject that was particularly popular at the time. The projects are designed with the beginner in mind, with simple step-by-steps to help you learn the basic skills needed. Once you have had a go at a few basic projects and mastered the techniques you will be ready to progress to bigger things – stools, chairs, a table perhaps.

Découpage may sound daunting to the beginner. But with a little patience and care the plainest of objects can be transformed into something exciting and creative. This book will help you on your way. Read and enjoy!

Materials

DÉCOUPAGE MATERIALS

PAPER

Victorian scraps were tailormade for découpage. 'Scrap' was the name given to sheets of die-cut and embossed chromo-lithographs. These images were of an astonishingly high quality. The accuracy of the die-cutting was such that scissors were barely needed at all.

Albums pasted up with collections of scrap became known as 'scrapbooks'. Queen Victoria herself is known to have been a keen scrapbook keeper. Scraps were also used to adorn screens, or 'scrapscreens'. This art form was particularly popular in Germany, Britain and the United States – indeed, one of the most famous manufacturers of scraps, Raphael Tuck, was based in Germany and New York.

Another art form using scraps and pictures that was a particular favourite with the Victorians was decalcomania. This involved gluing scraps to the inside of clear glass vessels – typically vases – and then coating them with whitewash or enamel.

We have chosen images that are ideal for the projects and in-keeping with the Victorian era, but there are endless supplies of prints and images available to suit all tastes – see the section on Sources and Suppliers for some useful addresses.

Books are of course an excellent source of material. Second-hand books and magazines in particular can yield all manner of pictures suitable for découpage. Similarly, remaindered or bargain books are a good source. Try the 'natural science' and 'history' sections.

Giftwrap and wallpaper is good for découpage. Choose only high-quality, thicker papers. These papers have the advantage of using repeated images, which is a great help for some projects. (See the section on Suppliers in this book for some useful addresses.)

Postcards can be used, but because of their thickness, it is often necessary to split the card using a razor blade or thumbnail. Alternatively, use more coats of varnish.

Magazines are a useful source, but again avoid those produced with cheaper paper. Newsprint is often unsuitable because of the ink on the reverse. Poke around in junk shops for bygone periodicals.

Photocopies are a brilliant way to plunder all kinds of archive, but check that you are not breaking any copyright on the material you are using and keep within the guidelines of the law. A good machine with quality paper will give you a high-quality black and white image for a fraction of the price of a print. Colour photocopies used to be of poorer quality but have now become just as good as black and white. Once again, repeat images are not a problem and cutting error need not be disastrous.

BLANKS

Blanks are the bases from which many items are made. It is possible to find blanks in many guises including hatboxes, candlesticks, table mats, novelty boxes and letter racks. These can be purchased either direct from a craft retailer or via mail order. Alternatively you may track down new 'unfinished' blanks at your local DIY store.

PAINTS, VARNISHES, BRUSHES

Here it is best to visit a specialist shop, where the precise materials required should be in stock (see the section on Suppliers in this book for some useful addresses). Many of the paint colours we have used for these projects come from the Farrow and Ball specialist paint range. Suppliers to the National Trust, Farrow and Ball produce excellent quality paints, many of which are replica historic colours. A wide range of sample pots are available from the manufacturer, which are ideal for smaller-scale projects.

Paint is used to colour bases, tint scraps and touch in designs. You can also use it to enhance a decoration – try turning your hand to painting scrolls or ribbons. Household emulsion paint is as good as anything for painting blanks. It is a good idea to buy a small selection of primary colours and then mix them as required. For finer work you will need to use good quality artists' watercolour or coloured pencils. Inks may be used too, but be careful, ink is a concentrated pigment! For some finishes, you will need artists' oil paint.

In this book we've used crackle varnish. This two-part varnish compound is readily available from craft shops or by mail order. It's easy to use and you will find it very effective in giving your object that mellowed, aged look. Look out for the Applicraft varnish, which is water-based and extremely easy to use.

We have also used scumble glaze medium. Again, this is available from good arts stockists or via mail order. Scumble medium mixes with paint and gives an opaque glaze to the surface of an object, which can be either smooth or distressed.

Other varnishes you will need to have to hand are acrylic water-based varnishes – we've used Craig and Rose – and a good quality oil-based varnish.

And last but not least, you will need a pot or two of gold and silver paste. We've used Rub and Buff wax paste, which gives excellent coverage and buffs to a deep shine. Again, you can buy these items from good quality craft shops or via mail order.

GLUE

The most commonly used glue in découpage is water-soluble PVA glue. This vinyl glue will stick paper, cardboard and fabric and can be diluted to any strength: a dilution of 1 part water to 5 parts glue makes for the most useful mixture. PVA glue is widely available.

SUNDRIES

While each project in this book lists the specific materials you'll need, there are a number of sundries that are common to all the découpage projects. You will need:

- Manicure scissors/découpage scissors. a craft knife or scalpel.
- Household scissors.
- Tweezers.
- A cutting mat and pasting board (a thick cardboard sheet works just as well).
- Repositioning adhesive such as Blu Tack.
- Disposable household cloth and natural sponge.
- HB pencil.
- Paper kitchen towels.
- White spirit for cleaning brushes with oil-based paint.
- Soap for cleaning glue brushes.
- Glass jars with screw tops – for storing varnish and glue mediums.

BRUSHES:

- Decorator's brushes – 1-inch and 2.5-inch – for painting on emulsion and applying glue.
- Varnishing brush – keep a dedicated varnishing brush set aside for varnishing.
- artists' brush – no. 4 – for those delicate touches.

SAFETY AND YOU

The following helpful hints should ensure trouble-free sessions at the découpage table:

•1• Make sure your working area is well-ventilated, dust free and uncluttered. Avoid using extension cables or anything that can be tripped over.

•2• Cover your work surface with newspaper when painting, gluing and varnishing.

•3• Always wear an apron. Never wear fibre-rich clothing such as wool – fibres soon find their way into paint and varnish.

•4• Wear thin, well-fitting rubber gloves when working with varnish. Wear gloves at all times if you have particularly sensitive skin.

•5• Keep all materials away from naked flame.

•6• If you are working on a number of projects, invest in a cheap paper dust mask. This will protect your lungs against dust and paint fumes.

Blackboard

Here is a project you might like to try with the children. All you need is a good-size piece of medium-density fibreboard (MDF), some paint, some pictures and just a little patience. Working with children can be very rewarding, so long as you don't get too bogged down in procedure and perfection. Let your young helpers have a little bit of fun – allow them to chose which teddies to use and let them do the cutting out, even if the scraps end up a bit rough around the edges. You can also let the children take charge of the gluing, so long as you keep a close eye on them. Of course, you will need to take control when it comes to varnishing.

Blackboards come in all shapes and sizes, so do not feel restricted. You could make a small desk-size blackboard that is just right for a child's work station, or go for something more mirror-size that can be hung on a wall. Another idea is a larger free-standing blackboard – again following the basic step-by-step below, then mounting the finished object on a sturdy free-standing easle frame.

WHAT YOU NEED

- One new piece of MDF, cut to size – we've used one that has been shaped at the top

- Masking tape

- Blackboard paint (available from any good DIY store)

- Bright yellow emulsion paint

- Teddy images

- PVA glue

- Water-based (acrylic) eggshell varnish

WHAT YOU DO

•1• Take a slightly moistened clean cloth and wipe over the surface of the MDF board to remove any dust.

•2• Paint the whole of the board with two coats of emulsion paint. Allow each coat to dry out thoroughly.

•3• When painting a large area, make sure you apply the paint in short strokes, working in all directions – you do not want to end up with the paint going all one way as this will create 'lines'.

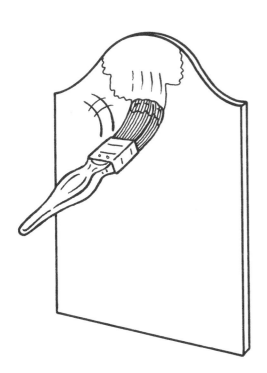

•4• Measure out a rectangle in the centre of the board – this is where the blackboard area will be. If you are not sure how much border to allow, try cutting out your rectangle area in paper first and position it on top of the painted board to see how well it looks.

•5• Stick masking tape along the outer edges of the marked-out area. Make sure it is well stuck down and that there are no gaps.

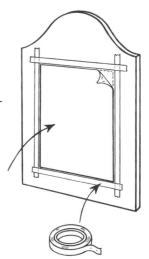

•6• Now you can paint the space you have made with two coats of blackboard paint (see manufacturer's instructions for drying times). Set aside until thoroughly dry, then carefully remove the masking tape.

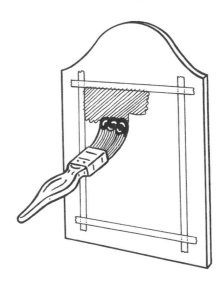

•7• Decide on the teddies you want to use as decoration. Cut them out as carefully as you can.

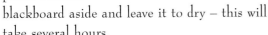

•8• Arrange them around the edge of the blackboard, then when you are happy that they are right, place them on a gluing board. Now apply enough glue to the backs of the motifs to ensure they can be well stuck down, carefully position them around the frame and gently firm them in place. Put the blackboard aside and leave it to dry – this will take several hours.

•9• Now apply three to four coats of acrylic eggshell varnish over the top of the découpaged blackboard frame. Make sure you do not get any on the blackboard paint, as this will effect the surface.

•10• Allow each coat of varnish to thoroughly dry before applying a further coat. (See manufacturer's instructions for recommended drying times.)

CD or Disk Storage Box

Here's something unusual that you might like to try – an original, handmade CD/disk box. Now you can dispense with your unsightly plastic computer disk filing system, that flimsy CD rack and all those shoe boxes wherein you keep everything that hasn't got a proper home. A découpage storage box looks good anywhere, whether its on the shelf in the office, on the bookcase in the sitting room or on a child's bedroom desk.

This project is simple and quick to do. Small storage boxes are relatively easy to get hold of – try the local DIY store, gift shop and craft outlet. You might also find a shoe box that is exactly the right size for CDs or tape cassettes.

- One blank CD/disk storage box

- Dark blue emulsion paint

- Pale stone emulsion paint (see Farrow & Ball range)

- Teddy bear images

- PVA glue

- Water-based (acrylic) matt varnish

- Silver wax paste

WHAT YOU DO

•1• Using a soft clean brush, sweep out the inside of the box to remove any dust. Rub down any blemishes on the outside of the box using fine sandpaper, then wipe over the outside with a clean damp cloth to take off the dust.

•2• Paint the inside of the box with two or three coats of dark blue emulsion paint, allowing the paint to dry thoroughly after each coat.

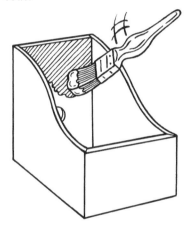

•3• When the inside is completely dry, paint the outside of the box with two coats of pale stone emulsion paint, once again allowing each coat to dry thoroughly.

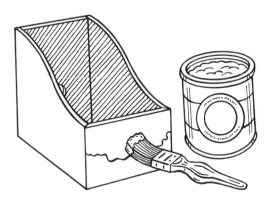

•4• Using a pair of sharp manicure scissors, carefully cut out the teddy bear images that you have selected from the back of this book.

•5• Place the teddies around the sides of the box until you are happy with the effect – you might find it useful to use a repositioning adhesive such as Blu Tack when arranging cut-outs on a vertical surface, as this will allow you to adjust the motifs easily until you are happy with the effect.

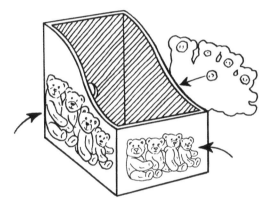

•6• Now place the scraps face down on a pasting board and coat with PVA/water-based acrylic glue.

•7• Carefully position them, then firm down, making sure all the edges are stuck, then set aside to dry – this will take several hours.

•8• Apply three or four coats of acrylic matt varnish to the entire surface area, allowing each coat to dry thoroughly before applying the next. Remember, the more coats of varnish that are applied, the longer the coats take to thoroughly dry.

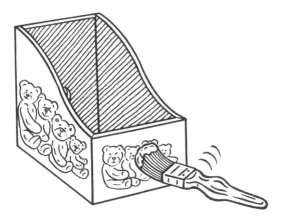

•9• Finally, using your finger apply a little silver wax paste to the top edge of the box. Set aside until the wax is completely dry, buff to shine, then fill up your box!

Double Letter Rack

A letter rack decorated with teddies makes the perfect gift for both young and old. Let your imagination run wild with this object. You can use any sort of teddy bear or toy image, matching your scraps to the base colour or offsetting them against a contrasting base colour to heighten the effect.

Letter rack blanks are a stock item for most craft suppliers. You may also be able to buy them from gift and stationery shops. A letter rack is easy to work with; all its surfaces are flat and smooth, making for easy adhesion.

WHAT YOU NEED

- One blank double letter rack

- Ochre emulsion paint (Farrow & Ball, Octagon Yellow)

- Acrylic scumble glaze (available from art shops and mail order suppliers)

- Artists' acrylic paint – burnt umber

- Teddy bear images

- PVA glue

- Water-based (for example, acrylic) eggshell varnish

- Gold wax paste

- Natural sponge

- Muslin cloth

WHAT YOU DO

•1• Using a soft clean brush, dust the letter rack blank to remove any residue dirt – you may need to rub down the larger flat surfaces lightly with fine-grade sandpaper to ensure they are completely smooth. Remember to wipe over any rubbed down surfaces with a damp cloth afterwards to remove the dust.

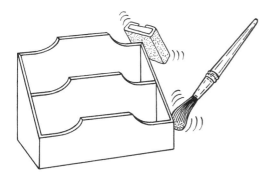

•2• Paint the entire surface with two coats of ochre emulsion paint. Allow the paint to dry thoroughly between coats.

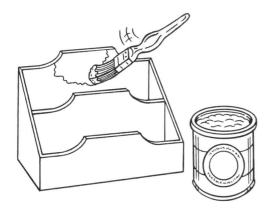

•3• Select the images you want to use and carefully cut them out.

•4• Put the images on to a pasting board and apply PVA glue to the backs. Now paste the images onto the letter rack.

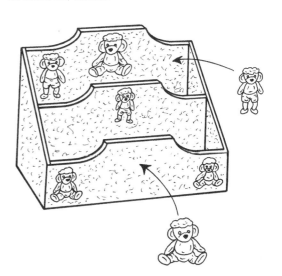

•5• Leave the rack to dry out – this will take at least 12 hours.

•6• On a plate mix a small amount of artists' acrylic paint, raw umber, with a small amount of scumble glaze and mix well. You are working to a ratio of 1 part paint to 2 parts scumble.

•7• Dampen the sponge and dab it into the glaze, squeezing it gently against the sides of the plate until the sponge has an even coating of glaze. Use some kitchen paper to dab out any surplus glaze.

•8• Now using a light dabbing motion, apply the glaze to the surface of the rack. It is a good idea to practise this application method first on a scrap of paper. What you are aiming at is a broken, textured surface that has no splodges!

•9• Leave until completely dry – this can take several hours.

•10• Now apply three or four coats of water-based/acrylic eggshell varnish to all the surfaces. You will need to allow each coat to dry thoroughly before applying the next – between three to six hours minimum.

•11• For a final touch, apply a tiny amount of gold wax paste to all the edges. Leave until dry – about 2 hours – then buff to shine.

Mini Chest

S torage can be a big problem in many
houses, and when
it comes to all those
little bits and pieces
there is never enough
room. This is where a
mini chest comes in
handy. Depending
on their size,
mini chests
can be used to
store all
manner of
miscellaneous items such as paper clips and
rubber bands, stamps and envelopes, receipts
and sales vouchers – just about anything you
know you'll lose if you put it anywhere else.

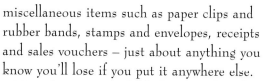

Mini chests are available from good quality
arts and crafts shops and mail order
catalogues, and also from some DIY stores
and interior furnishing centres. You could
also keep a look out for them in junk and
antique shops.

- One blank wooden mini chest

- Emulsion paint – you'll need four
  tones of one colour. We've used sand,
  cream, lemon and yellow.

- Teddy bear images

- PVA glue

- Water-based (acrylic) eggshell varnish

WHAT YOU DO

•1• Remove the drawers from the chest and clean all the surfaces to remove any dust and dirt. You may want to rub down any rough surfaces with fine glass-paper.

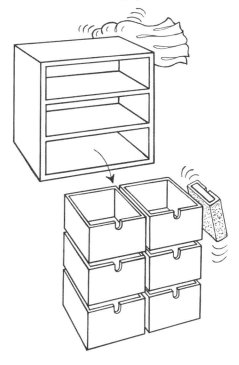

•2• Paint the outside surface of the chest with two coats of the darkest shade of emulsion paint, allowing the paint to dry thoroughly after each coat.

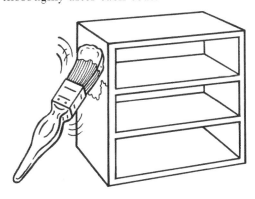

•3• Paint the drawers two at a time, using a different shade of emulsion paint for each pair. Again, you will need to apply two coats, allowing each coat to dry out thoroughly.

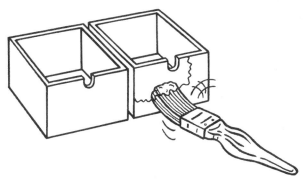

•4• Now select your teddy bear images and carefully cut them out. Arrange them on the drawer fronts until you are happy with the effect – you may find spot-gluing them in place helps you to visualize the design.

•5• Once you are happy with the design, place your scraps on a pasting board right sides down and paste them up with PVA adhesive.

•6• Glue the images into position on the fronts of the drawers, making sure all the edges are well stuck down and that you have pressed out any air bubbles.

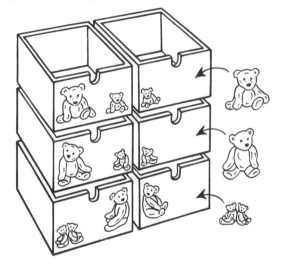

•7• Set aside and leave the drawers to dry – this can take up to twelve hours (leaving overnight is best).

•8• Finally, apply at least four coats of acrylic eggshell varnish to all the painted surfaces.

•9• Make sure each coat is thoroughly dry before applying the next – a minimum of two hours between coats is probably all that is necessary, although you may find that the third and fourth coats take longer to dry.

•10• When every surface is completely dry, put the drawers back in the chest and stand back and enjoy the effect.

Pencil Box

If a child likes colouring and drawing then they will enjoy looking after their pencils and crayons. For the devoted young artist what could be a more perfect gift than the pencil box we've made here, especially if your young friend also happens to like teddy bears as well!

Another idea you might like to try is matching pencil holders. These can be made from all sorts of discarded household cardboard items such as tall box containers, tumblers and tubes. All you need to do is select several containers, each a different size, and transform them using the same basic method as the one given below. After you have completed your découpage, simply group the containers together and stick in place using a strong contact adhesive.

WHAT YOU NEED

- One blank wooden pencil box (available from any good craft shop or mail order supplier)

- Off-white emulsion paint

- Blue emulsion paint

- Acrylic scumble glaze medium (available from any good art or craft shop or mail order supplier)

- Teddy bear images

- PVA glue

- Water-based (acrylic) matt varnish

WHAT YOU DO

•1• Clean the surface of the pencil box with a soft brush to remove any dust and dirt.

•2• Paint the entire surface with two or three coats of off-white emulsion paint, allowing the paint to dry thoroughly after each coat.

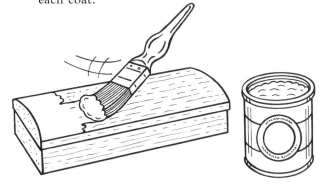

•3• Mix one teaspoon of scumble glaze medium with the same amount of blue emulsion paint.

•4• Using a paintbrush, cover the entire box with the glaze mixture. Now dab the surface all over with the end of the same paintbrush to create a stippled, textured effect. Set aside and leave until completely dry. This will take several hours.

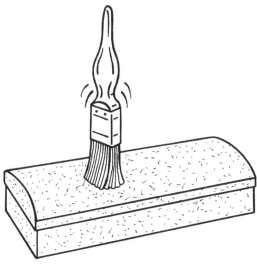

•5• Choose your images and carefully cut them out. Place them on the lid of the box until you are happy with the effect.

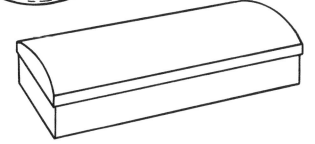

•6• Once you are happy with your arrangement, paste the scraps into position using PVA/water-based acrylic glue. Set aside to dry – this will take several hours.

•7• Apply three or four coats of acrylic matt varnish to the entire surface area, allowing each coat to dry thoroughly before applying the next. Remember, the more coats of varnish that are applied, the longer the coats take to thoroughly dry.

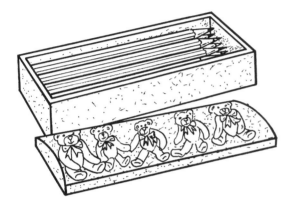

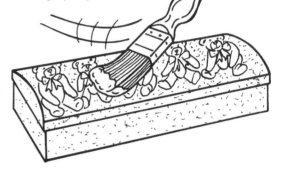

•8• Finally, fill your box with some favourite pencils and pens!

Decorative Wall Shelf

Découpage can make the plainest object into something special, quite literally transforming it into a thing of unique beauty. An otherwise ordinary piece of furniture, for example this simple wall shelf, can be made to look like something everyone simply 'must have'.

Once you have mastered the basic techniques, you will be keen to start on some household furniture items. It is a good idea to have a go at something simple first, however, and this project is just the place to begin. Having built up your confidence, you might like to move on to some matching items, such as a toy box or a child's chair.

We've used a new plywood shelf for this project, but don't feel you have to do the same. You may have some old shelving of your own that would do just as well. When using second-hand furniture, make sure the surfaces are well prepared before you start. Sand down any old painted surfaces to form a 'key' for the new paint, and thoroughly clean all the surfaces with sugar soap to remove any grease or dirt.

WHAT YOU NEED

- One blank plywood shelf (search art and craft shops and mail order suppliers for a design you like)

- Off-white emulsion paint

- Pale grey emulsion paint (see Farrow & Ball range)

- Acrylic scumble glaze (available from art shops and mail order suppliers)

- A selection of teddy bear images

- PVA glue

- Red acrylic paint

- Water-based (for example, acrylic) matt varnish

- Gold wax paste

WHAT YOU DO

•1• Thoroughly clean the shelf to remove any dust. Use fine-grade sandpaper to rub down any rough surfaces. Wipe away any remaining dust with a damp cloth.

•2• Paint the shelf with two coats off-white emulsion paint. Allow the paint to dry thoroughly between coats.

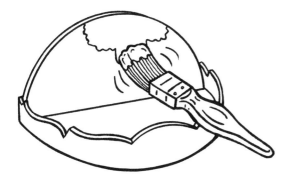

•3• When painting, work the paint in short cross-hatch strokes to ensure even coverage: do not be tempted to brush all one way.

•4• Paint the inner shelf area with one coat of pale grey emulsion paint. Set aside until the paint is completely dry.

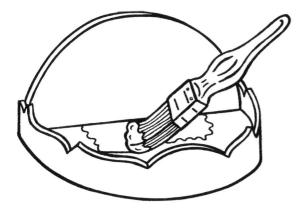

•5• On a plate mix a half a tablespoon of pale grey emulsion paint with two tablespoons of scumble glaze and mix well – the consistency you require is rather like that of single cream.

•6• Carefully paint the glaze on to the front faces of the shelf using a small one-inch household paintbrush.

•7• Wipe the brush on a piece of cloth to remove any surplus paint, then stipple the surfaces that you have just painted by gently dabbing the end of the brush over the glaze.

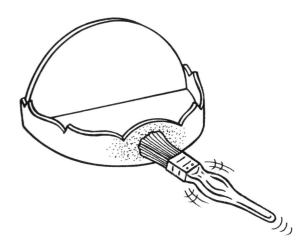

•8• Leave until completely dry – this can take several hours.

•9• Now select your teddy bear images. You might find you will need to enlarge some of the images from the back of this book to make them more suitable for the object you are working on. This can be done quite simply using a colour photocopier.

•10• Having chosen your teddies, place them on a cutting board and carefully cut them out using a sharp craft knife.

•11• Apply PVA glue to the backs of the images and position them. Firm them in place using a clean dry cloth, then set the shelf aside until the glue is completely dry – this can take at least 12 hours.

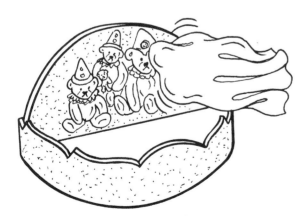

•12• Now, using an artists' paintbrush and a little acrylic paint, carefully paint around the front edge to highlight (see picture).

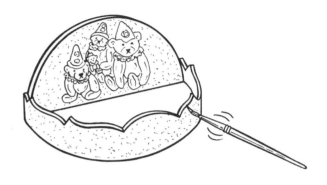

•13• Lastly, apply three or four coats of water-based/acrylic matt varnish over all surfaces to seal. You will need to allow each coat to dry thoroughly before applying the next – between three and six hours minimum.

•14• Once dry, apply a little gold wax paste along the upper edges to complete the effect.

Wastepaper Bin

Here is an easy project which should help build up your confidence. A wastepaper bin may not be the prettiest item in a room, but with a modest découpage make-over it can be transformed into something distinctive and eye-catching.

We have selected an MDF wastepaper bin for this project. MDF, or medium-density fibreboard, has a surface that is rather like fine chipboard; it is ideal for découpage as it is flat and even and requires minimal initial preparation.

WHAT YOU NEED

- One blank MDF wastepaper bin (available from any good craft shop or DIY store)

- Deep red emulsion paint (see Farrow & Ball range)

- Fox red emulsion paint (see Farrow & Ball range)

- Acrylic scumble glaze medium (available from any good art or craft shop or mail order supplier)

- Disposable household cloth

- Teddy images

- PVA glue

- Water-based (acrylic) eggshell varnish

- Gold wax paste

40

WHAT YOU DO

•1• Clean the surface of the wastepaper bin with a soft brush to remove any dust and dirt; you may find a damp sponge works best.

•2• Paint the inside of the bin with two coats of fox red emulsion paint, allowing the paint to dry thoroughly after each coat (this will take between two and four hours).

•3• Paint the outside of the bin with two coats of deep red emulsion paint, once again allowing each coat to thoroughly dry.

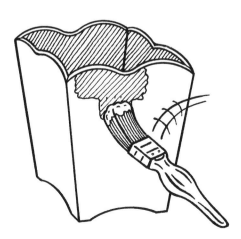

•4• Mix one tablespoon of fox red emulsion paint with three tablespoons of scumble glaze medium and mix until you have a smooth, thick consistency.

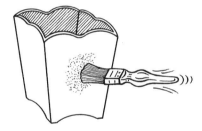

•5• Apply the glaze mix to the entire outer surface of the bin using a one-inch household paint brush: it is advisable to paint the whole of one face first before moving on to the next.

•6• When you have painted all the faces, lightly stipple the entire surface with the end of the paintbrush to eliminate any brush strokes (make sure the paintbrush is free of any surplus paint).

•7• Now slightly dampen the disposable cleaning cloth and roll it up into a long sausage shape. Carefully roll the sausage diagonally across all four surfaces until a you have a subtle stippled effect. When you have achieved this effect, set the bin aside until it is completely dry.

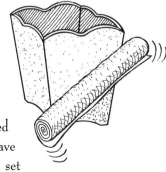

•8• Choose the teddy images you wish to use and carefully cut them out. You may like to enlarge some of the images from the back of this book to give a more striking impact.

•9• Once chosen, position your teddies until you are happy with the effect.

•10• Paste the scraps into position using PVA/water-based acrylic glue. Set aside to dry – this will take several hours.

•11• Apply three or four coats of acrylic eggshell varnish to the entire surface area, allowing each coat to dry thoroughly before applying the next. Remember, the more coats of varnish that are applied, the longer the coats take to thoroughly dry.

•12• Finally, apply a little gold wax paste to the rim of the wastepaper bin for a final decorative touch.

Small Planter

This stylish planter would look good just about anywhere in the house, and although it's a planter it doesn't necessarily have to be used to display plants. You might find it looks rather good filled with a display of dried flowers.

Planters come in all sorts of shapes and sizes and in a variety of materials. The one we are using is made of medium-density fibreboard, which is extremely easy to work with. You might find a galvanised metal planter instead. If this is the case, then simply give the metal a generous coat of metal primer first before applying the emulsion paint base colour.

This project would make an excellent gift idea. After all, everyone loves a teddy!

WHAT YOU NEED

- One small MDF planter (the one used here comes from a craft stockist)

- Black emulsion paint

- Cream emulsion paint

- A selection of teddy images

- PVA glue

- Oil-based eggshell varnish

- Two-part crackle varnish (large cracks base coat and top coat)

- Artist's oil paint – raw umber

- Small piece of muslin cloth

- White spirit

- Gold wax paste

WHAT YOU DO

•1• Using a soft, slightly damp cloth, wipe over the inside and outside of the planter to remove any dust.

•2• Paint the inside of the container with a coat of black emulsion paint. Set aside to dry, then paint again.

•3• Now paint the outside of the planter with two coats of cream emulsion paint, again setting aside to dry after each application.

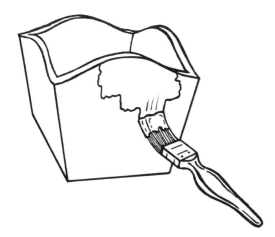

•4• Select the images you want to use – we've used one large teddy image for the front face of the planter and one smaller teddy image for the corresponding inside face.

•5• Carefully cut out your motifs place them on a pasting board. Apply PVA glue to the backs, making sure not to over-glue. Position carefully and firm in place.

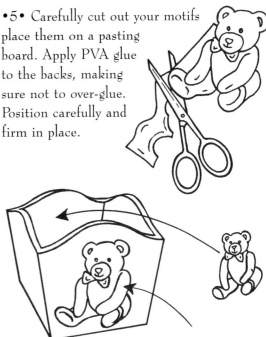

•6• Leave to dry (you may need to leave overnight).

•7• Next paint on two coats of the crackle varnish base coat to the outside surface, allowing the first coat to dry completely before applying the second.

•8• When varnishing make sure your working area is well ventilated and as dust free as possible. Keep a brush set aside especially for varnishing and look after it well – you don't want stray hairs in the varnish!

•9• When the second coat is dry, apply an even layer of crackle varnish top coat. You may find it necessary to warm the pot slightly by standing it in a shallow bowl of warm water, as this will make the varnish easier to spread.

•10• You now need to wait for the top coat to dry – this may take some time (anything from 6 to 24 hours), so be patient! As time goes on, a layer of fine cracks will appear on the surface.

•11• Dampen the muslin cloth with white spirit and squeeze out a pea-size amount of raw umber oil paint onto it. Rub the pigment over the crackle varnish and watch as the cracks are revealed. Make sure not to use too much paint.

•12• Wipe away any excess paint using a clean dry piece of muslin, then set the boxes aside for a further 72 hours until completely dry, making sure to leave them in a cool, well ventilated room.

•13• Apply a thin coat of oil-based eggshell varnish over all the surfaces. This will protect the boxes and make sure the crackle varnish is not damaged.

•14• Lastly, apply a little gold wax paste with your finger to the top edge of the planter to complete the effect.

Candle Shade

Lampshade découpage is particularly satisfying. Not only is it relatively easy to do, it provides the most wonderful effect when finished and illuminated. Candle shades and sticks are readily available. The sticks come in wood, metal and MDF, the shades in metal, cotton or card.

Currently extremely popular, several commercial companies now specialise in producing découpage lamps. So why not save yourself some money (the same products retail at surprisingly high prices today, both in the UK and the United States) and have a go at making your own unique one.

WHAT YOU NEED

• One blank card shade – white or cream (you might like to make a matching pair, in which case you'll need two)

• Yellow emulsion paint

• Acrylic scumble glaze (available from art shops and mail order suppliers)

• Teddy images

• PVA glue

• Water-based (for example, acrylic) matt varnish

WHAT YOU DO

•1• On a saucer or plate mix equal quantities of acrylic scumble glaze and yellow emulsion to form a glaze. (A stiff brush or spoon is the best mixing tool.)

•2• Now carefully paint the glaze onto the surface of the shade, starting at the top and creating concentric rings that become wider the further down the shade you go.

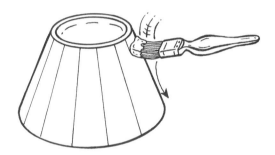

•3• This will take a little practice to perfect, so make sure you are confident before starting on the shade itself. It is a good idea to practice the technique first on paper, to make sure you have mastered how to graduate the lines

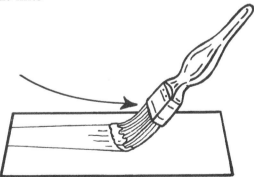

- you might find that faintly marking out the line widths in pencil first will help. You will also need to remember to press down the paintbrush harder as you move down the shade and your rings become wider.

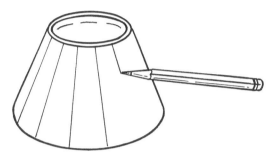

•4• Leave until completely dry – this can take several hours.

•5• Select the teddy images that you want to use and carefully cut them out.

•6• Put the images on to a pasting board and apply PVA glue to the backs. Now paste the images onto the surface of the shade and firm in place. You may find that some images will not lie completely flat, in which case a few tiny snips here and there around the motif should allow you to ease it into place.

•7• Leave the shade to dry out – this will take at least 12 hours.

•8• Finally apply three or four coats of water-based/acrylic matt varnish to both sides of the shade. You will need to allow each coat to dry thoroughly before applying the next – between three and six hours minimum.

•9• Your candle shade is now ready to be fitted onto its holder, ready for illuminating.

Mirror

Mirrors often find their way into second-hand/junk shops, where they can be bought for next to nothing. Here's an idea for giving one a new lease of life. And of course you need not stop at a mirror. Why not découpage a matching pair of candles, or a jug and basin set.

For the project below we've used a blank wooden mirror frame, which needs only minimal preparation. If, however, you are going to make-over an old mirror frame you will need to thoroughly clean it first using sandpaper to remove any flaking paint and varnish and sugar soap to clean off any dirt or grease.

52

WHAT YOU DO

•1• Remove the mirror from the frame and set to one side. Prepare the frame, rubbing down any rough edges and cleaning where necessary. Finally, wipe over with a damp cloth to remove any dust.

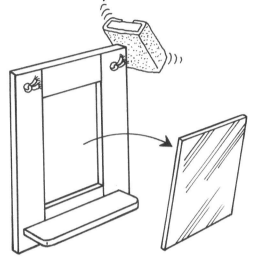

•2• Paint the whole of the frame with two coats of deep red emulsion paint, allowing to paint to dry thoroughly after each coat.

•3• Rub the surface of the frame all over with candle wax, concentrating on the edges where normal wear and tear would occur.

•4• Now paint over the surface again, this time with two coats of bright white emulsion paint. Again, allow the paint to dry after each coat.

•5• Once the second coat is dry, rub the surface gently with wire wool until areas of the paint come away to reveal a glimpse of the red emulsion beneath. Take care not to rub too enthusiastically, you are after a slightly distressed look, not large areas of exposed red paint.

•6• Wipe carefully with a damp cloth to remove the dust.

•7• Choose your teddy bear images and carefully cut them out. Try them out on the front face of the frame to make sure they will 'work' – you may find smaller images are best.

•8• Once you are happy with your arrangement, paste the scraps into position using PVA/water-based acrylic glue. Set aside to dry – this will take several hours.

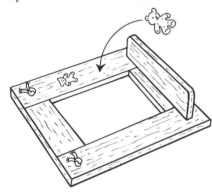

•9• Now three or four coats of acrylic matt varnish to the entire surface area, allowing each coat to dry thoroughly before applying the next. Remember, the more coats of varnish that are applied, the longer the coats take to thoroughly dry.

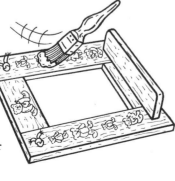

•10• And finally, a coat of dark brown furniture polish, sparingly applied, allowed to dry and then buffed, will add a discreetly aged look to the frame.

•11• When the frame is completely dry, replace the mirror and fix into position. Hang in place, stand back and enjoy!

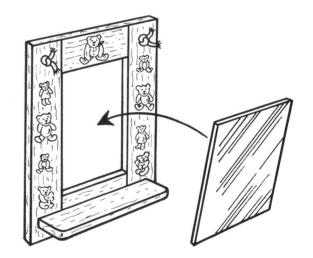

Sources and Suppliers

PAPER – UNITED KINGDOM

The suppliers listed below are useful sources for Victorian scraps, fine art giftwrap, fine art wallpaper, print-room borders and decoration and copyright-free designs.

Caspari Ltd
9 Shire Hill
Saffron Walden
Essex CB11 3AP
tel.: 01799 513010

The Dover Bookshop
18 Earlham Street
London WC2H 9LN
tel.: 0207 836 2111
Many of the images and scraps used in the projects in this book were reproduced by the kind permission of Dover publications.

Falkiner Fine Papers Ltd
76 Southampton Row
London WC1B 4AR
tel.: 0207 831 1151

Liberty and Co.
Regent Street
London WI
tel.: 0207 734 1234

Mamelok Press
Northern Way
Bury St Edmunds
Suffolk IP32 6NJ
tel.: 01284 762291

National Gallery Publications Ltd
5-9 Pall Mall East
London SW17 5BA
tel.: 0207 839 8544

National Trust Enterprises Ltd
36 Queen Anne's Gate
London SW1H 9AS
tel.: 0207 222 9251
(see also National Trust shops nationwide)

Paperchase Products Ltd
213 Tottenham Court Road
London W1P 9AF
tel.: 0207 323 3703

Past Times
Witney
Oxford OX8 6BH
tel.: 01993 770440
(see also Past Times shops nationwide)

A. J. Sanderson Ltd
52 Berners Street
London WI
tel.: 0207 584 3344

Scumble Goosie
Toadsmoor Road
Stroud
Gloucestershire GL5 2TB
tel.: 01453 731305

PAPER – UNITED STATES AND CANADA

Brandon Memorabilia
PO Box 20165
New York NY 10011
USA

Brunschwig & Fils
379 3rd Avenue
New York NY 10022
USA

Dover Publications
31 East 2nd Street
Mineola
NY 11501
USA
tel.: 001 516 294 7000

Flax Artists Materials
PO Box 7216
San Francisco
CA 94120-7216
USA
tel.: 001 415 468 7530

Laila's
1136 Lorimar Drive
Mississauga
Ontario L5S 1RY
Canada
tel.: 001 905 795 8955

Ornamenta
c/o C. Hyland
979 3rd Avenue
New York NY 10022
USA

A. J. Sanderson Ltd
979 3rd Avenue
New York NY 10022
USA

PAINTS, FINISHES AND TOOLS – UNITED KINGDOM

The suppliers listed below are useful sources for specialist fine art materials such as paint, pigments, brushes, sealers, primers, glue, varnishes and specialist sundries.

L. Cornelissen & Son Ltd
105 Great Russell Street
London WC1B 3LA
tel.: 0207 636 1045

Daler-Rowney Ltd
12 Percy Street
London W1A 2BP
tel.: 0207 636 8241

Farrow & Ball Ltd
Uddens Trading Estate
Wimborne
Dorset BH21 7NL
tel.: 01202 876 141

Foxwell and James
57 Farringdon Road
London EC1M 3JB
tel.: 0207 405 0152

J. H. Ratcliffe
135a Linaker Street
Southport PR8 DF
tel.: 01704 537999

Stuart R. Stevenson
68 Clerkenwell Road
London EC1M 5QA
tel.: 0207 253 1693

PAINTS, FINISHES AND TOOLS – UNITED STATES AND CANADA

Constantines
2050 East Chester Road
Bronx NY 10461
USA
tel.: 001 800 223 8087

Garrett Wade
161 Avenue of Americas
New York NY 10013
USA
tel.: 001 212 807 1155

Omer De Serres
334 Ste-Catherine East
Montreal
Quebec H2X IL7
Canada
tel.: 001 800 363 0318

Pearl Paint
308 Canal Street
New York NY 10013
USA
tel.: 001 800 221 6845

Sherwin Williams Canada, Inc.
170 Brunel Road
Mississanga
Ontario L4Z 1T5

Suppliers – Australia and New Zealand

Aidax Industries
64-68 Violet Street
Revesby
Sydney NSW 2212
Australia

Bristol Decorator Centre
76 Oatley Court
Belconnen ACT 2617
New Zealand

Golding Handcraft Centre
161 Cuba Street
PO Box 9022
Wellington
New Zealand

Oxford Art Supplies Pty Ltd
221-223 Oxford Street
Darlinhurst NSW 2010
Australia

Mail-order – United Kingdom

Mail-order companies are good sources of blanks, general craft sundries and fine art materials. Here are some useful addresses.

Fred Aldous
37 Lever Street
Manchester M60 1UX
tel.: 0161 236 2477
(arts and crafts)

The Box, Blank and Plaque Co.
D & S Crafts
Little Swineside
West Scafton
Leyburn
N. Yorks DL8 4RU
tel.: 01969 640617

Crafts and Collectables
1 Station Way
Cheam
Surrey SM3 8SD
tel.: 0208 288 0601
(arts and crafts)

Dainty Supplies Ltd
Unit 3
Phoenix Road
Crowther Ind. Est.
Washington
Tyne and Wear NE38 0AD
tel.: 0191 416 7886
(arts and crafts)

Janik Ltd
Brickfield Lane
Ruthin
North Wales LL15 2TN
tel.: 01824 702096
(arts and crafts)

MSA Crafts
Marvic House
Graingers Lane
Cradley Heath
West Midlands B64 6AD
tel.: 01384 568790
(arts and crafts)

Myriad Designs
PO Box 1
Prenton DO
Wirral L43 6XZ
tel.: 0151 652 5174
(blanks)

Smithcraft
Unit 1
Eastern Road
Aldershot
Hants GU12 4TE
tel.: 01252 342626
(arts and crafts)

Useful contacts

Various craft organisations exist to help and support craftsmakers, both novices and the more experienced. Here are some useful addresses.

The Crafts Council
44a Pentonville Road
Islington
London N1 9BY
tel.: 0207 278 7700

(This nationwide organisation is a good place to start if you want to find out details of crafts societies and associations that exist locally. Alternatively, contact your Regional Arts Board, who hold databases of artists and associations and should be able to put you in touch with any local makers.)

Guild of British Découpeurs
18 Pembridge Close
Charlton Kings
Cheltenham GL5 6XY
tel.: 01242 235302

(Nationwide association which hosts regular meetings, workshops and exhibitions. Also produces bi-monthly magazine.)

National Guild of Découpeurs
5598 Forest View Drive
West Bend WI 53095
USA

(Worldwide organisation with chapters in Great Britain (listed above), South Africa, Australia, Canada and Japan.)